TEENA RAFFA-MULLIGAN

SEA SONG PUBLICATIONS / AUSTRALIA

Copyright © 2021 Teena Raffa-Mulligan.

All rights reserved. No part of this publication may be reproduced, distributed or transmitted in any form or by any means, including photocopying, recording, or other electronic or mechanical methods, without the prior written permission of the publisher, except in the case of brief quotations embodied in critical reviews and certain other noncommercial uses permitted by copyright law. For permission requests, contact the publisher.

Sea Song Publications

Warnbro

Western Australia

sea-song@bigpond.com

Raffa-Mulligan/ Teena

Author — First Edition

ISBN (softcover) 978-0-6485346-6-2

ISBN (ebook) 978-0-6485346-4-5

For every kid who'd like to take a story writing adventure but can't seem to get started.

CONTENTS

Start Your Story Adventure 1

Talking Stories 5

Cultivating Ideas 10

Plots and Plans 23

Word Pictures 42

Making Writing Exciting 49

What Sort of Story? 64

Who's Telling the Story? 74

Let's Begin 83

Carry On 88

...The End 96

Help Wanted 103

Pruning and Shaping 108

Imagination Unlimited 118

Stories are for Sharing 123

Finally 128

· 1 ·

START YOUR STORY ADVENTURE

THERE IS MAGIC IN stories. An expertly told story can cast a spell on its listeners. A well-written story will keep its readers enthralled from start to finish. Stories can excite and delight us, make us cry or laugh out loud. They can open our hearts and minds and help us to see situations differently. Stories give us a window into other worlds and help us to better understand our own world and our place in it.

Telling stories has been part of human life from earliest times. At first the tales were told around evening campfires or beneath the shelter of shady trees in the heat of the day. They were passed on from person to person. Some folk travelled the countryside sharing their stories with all who would listen. Later, stories were written on blocks of stone, then papyrus and eventually paper. The invention of printing presses made it easier to spread stories. Then came computers and digital technology and now we can read books on our screens, tablets or phones.

The ways we share stories have changed but one thing never does: our love of storytelling. As long as there are stories to tell, there will be writers.

Anyone who has a story to share can be a writer, including you. The only thing that ever stops us from writing stories is the thought that we can't. The fastest runners, the best players on the field, the kids who turn triple back flips with ease or dive like dolphins *believe* they can do it.

We don't tell ourselves that talking to each other is too hard. We simply do it. Yet many people believe writing stories is difficult so they don't even try. They are defeated before they start.

That's fine for those who don't want to write stories and are quite happy to paint pictures, play music, dance or do another creative activity instead. It is a problem for people who know they have a story — or more — to share but are stuck on the idea that it's too hard.

Instead of telling yourself, 'I can't write stories, I'm not a writer,' give yourself the clear message, 'I'm a writer, I *can* write stories.'

The next step is to think of writing as a journey. It starts with a single word written on paper or keyed into the computer. Once you set out, you have no idea where it will take you and what exciting things will happen along the way. That's the adventure.

Sometimes we need a kick start to head off in a new direction. This book is a fun, simple way to get you started writing stories.

.2.

TALKING STORIES

WRITING STORIES IS FUN! You get to create characters, put them in weird and wonderful situations and then decide what happens next. In your imagination you can be anyone, go anywhere and do anything at all. What will you be today? A super hero? A detective? An astronaut? Where will you go? Deep beneath the sea? To the top of the world's highest mountain? To the farthest stars? It's up to you!

I knew I wanted to be a writer from the time I learnt to read. Books excite me. They take me to other worlds and give me a window on experiences I don't have in my everyday life. I get to lose myself in the story.

As a kid I always had my nose in a book. I hid in Dad's parked car in the driveway at home so I could read without Mum asking me to help out around the house. When I wasn't reading I was writing. My head was full of stories and I couldn't write fast enough to get all the wonderful words down on paper. Not everyone finds writing stories that easy.

Yet everyone TELLS stories. You do too, though you might not realise it. You tell your friends where you've been and what you've been doing. Mum hears about your spectacular mark in the footie final, or the winning goal you shot from the very edge of the court. Dad hears how you felt when you got in trouble at school in front of the whole class for not paying attention. A family camping holiday, the awesome party planned for your next birthday, or the possum that's made a home in the roof are all stories to share with friends.

You might not find writing stories as easy as telling them. Even professional writers sometimes find it difficult to write the story they want to share. The difference is, they know HOW to write stories.

You can, too.

- ☑ People tell each other stories every day.
- ☑ Write down some of these stories and your storytelling becomes story writing.
- ☑ Writing stories is talking on paper.

 **TRY THIS...**

1. Next time you are with a group of friends, listen to the conversation instead of joining in. Think about what stories are being told. Briefly write down one of them later in the day.

2. You have some great news for your best friend. Before you pick up your phone to share it, take a few minutes to write it down first.

· 3 ·

CULTIVATING IDEAS

THE SEEDS OF YOUR STORIES

IDEAS ARE THE SEEDS of your stories. They may be planted any time of the day or night, no matter what you are doing. Given the right conditions, they will grow.

Just like a gardener you can weed out any ideas that are too weak to grow into a strong story and concentrate on those with the most potential. No writer could possibly have the time to write a story for every single idea that suggested itself. But you do want to encourage as many ideas as possible.

HELPING IDEAS TO GROW

IF YOU DECIDED TO grow peas in your back garden, you wouldn't sow the seeds, then neglect them until you felt hungry. Seeds only bear fruit given time and the right conditions so you'd do your best to provide these.

Encouraging your story ideas to grow is a little like gardening. Quite often ideas are very vague to begin with. Many are little more than fleeting thoughts. They are there and they have possibilities, but they need the right kind of conditions to develop into stories. Sometimes if the idea is very hardy, all it needs is time. Often, however, time only allows ideas to wither and die. To prevent that happening, you can fertilise them with questions.

QUESTIONS AS FERTILISER

THE IDEA FOR THIS book came to me while I was working with some Year Seven students during their creative writing sessions and learned how much difficulty they were having with their stories. It grew only because I asked myself how I could make story writing easier for them.

Asking yourself questions about your ideas helps them to develop so you can use them.

Perhaps you are going home from school on the bus one day when you overhear a conversation in the seat behind you.

Two women are talking about someone called Lisa being 'green with envy' because her ex-boyfriend just took his new girlfriend on a round the world cruise. It gives you an idea for a story: What if Lisa actually did turn green?

Take that first simple idea and see how big you can encourage it to grow. To do this, ask yourself questions.

Why did Lisa turn green? And who *is* Lisa? Forget the rest of the conversation. Invent your own character, and you will need to get to know this character very well.

What do they look like? Where do they live? What sort of person are they? Are they a person?

You need to know the same things about your story character as you know about yourself. Then you have to work out why they turned green, and what is going to happen next. How do they feel? How would you feel, if it were you? How your character reacts will decide what they do about turning green.

What about the process of turning green? Is it sudden and total — or gradual, from the toes up, soaking up the colour like blotting paper?

There must be other people in your story. Who are they and how do they react?

By the time you have given your idea this kind of attention, it should have burst into full bloom. Now you can use it.

In my chapter book, *The Find*, strange things happen to Jake when he takes home a mysterious object he found at the beach. Jake and his three cousins don't want the grownups to find out he seems to be turning into an alien. What will happen in your story?

It doesn't matter what suggests an idea in the first place. Sometimes you may never be able to identify the trigger. It's what you make of it that will result in a story only you could have written.

RECYCLING IDEAS

SOME IDEAS HAVE BEEN used time and again. There are countless stories about ghosts and haunted houses, dragons, time machines, outer space, solving mysteries and finding hidden treasure. Many use a dream to explain away a fantastic adventure.

These themes are so popular, they will continue to be used. Sometimes you will want to use them yourself. When you do, try to make your story different in some way.

A. Approach it from a new or unexpected angle.

Write your outer space story as if you are the alien. Our space ships would be UFOs to them. What would an alien do if an earthling suddenly arrived in its back yard?

B. Make your characters different.

Give your ghost a fear of people.

I gave my dragon an appetite for frozen peas and crossword puzzles and let it arrive from Jupiter on a seven-day tour to complicate life for a 10-year-old boy. What can you do with yours?

It's completely up to you. What you are doing is taking a new look at an old idea.

USING YOU

EVEN IF YOU THINK you can't come up with any ideas, you can still write stories by using what has actually happened rather than what could have happened.

You have a unique viewpoint on life. No one else will see things in quite the way you do or have identical experiences. How do you feel? What do you think? What has been happening to you up to today?

Have you ever been lost? Have you been on an interesting holiday, or appeared on TV?

What is the funniest thing that has ever happened to you? The most terrifying? The saddest?

One of the most moving stories I ever read during a creative writing session was written by a little girl who simply wrote down how she felt when her mother died. It made me cry.

Everyone has a story to tell. Quite often these personal stories are the most interesting of all because they are about real people.

WHAT you write about is not as important as HOW you write about it.

- [x] Ideas are the seeds of stories. They can be planted at any time and will grow given the right conditions.
- [x] Questions can fertilise ideas and help them to grow.
- [x] Old ideas can be recycled to produce new stories.
- [x] Personal experience can provide lots of story ideas.

 **TRY THIS...**

1. Plant some seeds for stories. An excellent way of triggering ideas is the What if? approach. Begin with something that has actually happened.

> **A.** Perhaps Mum has left you home for ten or 20 minutes while she does some shopping. You are all alone. Let your imagination take a little exercise and ask yourself some questions:
> What if she never came home?
> What if a stranger came to the front door?

What if your baby sister was left in your care, found the matches and set the kitchen curtains alight while you were watching the cartoons on TV? What would you do?

B. Maybe you've just taken your little brother to a birthday party.

What if you came back to collect him later and someone you'd never seen before answered the door? And that person said there weren't any children there, there hadn't been a party, and you must be mistaken. You know it is the house where you left your little brother two hours earlier. There were children there then. Where are they now? And where is your brother? What happens next?

You are taking something simple and asking yourself what would happen if an unexpected event complicated the situation. The possibilities are limited only by your imagination. Your imagination needs plenty of exercise to build it up and make it stronger in the same way your legs do. The more you use it and the more stimulation it has, the more active it becomes.

2. Keep an ideas book. Jot down any ideas you have as you think of them, or as soon as possible afterwards.

> Perhaps you are having a shower or walking to a friend's home and suddenly, there it is — the first sentence of a story. Or even the last. You have no idea what comes next or has gone before, but you like the sound of it. Store it for future use, like a squirrel hoarding nuts.
>
> Maybe a whole line of poetry is running through your mind as you play ball or jump rope. It isn't a part of anything yet, only an odd piece of a jigsaw puzzle waiting to be slotted into the right spot at some other

time. If you let it escape, you will never catch it later.

Your ideas book is just for you. Keep it small, so it can fit in your pocket or bag. Take it with you.

· 4 ·

PLOTS AND PLANS

IF BILL AND JENNY Jones decide to build a home on their block, they don't simply arrive one day with a truckload of bricks, tiles, doorframes, windows and concrete and launch right into the project. Everything about their house is planned down to the final detail long before the concrete floor is poured.

If you are going to build a story from one of your ideas it helps to have a plan. Your storyplan doesn't have to be as exact and complete as a houseplan. You don't always have to know what size your finished story will be, or every detail of conversation and action it will include. But you do need to have a general idea of the type of story it is, who the characters are and how the action is going to unfold. You have to know what happens.

DO WRITERS USE PLANS?

SOME WRITERS WILL TELL you they never use a plan or outline but simply sit down and start writing. It can be that easy and when it is, it's almost as if the story has written itself and all the writer had to do was hold the pen or operate the keyboard. Afterwards there can even be the feeling, 'Wow! Did I write that?'

If writing were always so easy it would be wonderful. Unfortunately it isn't, even for people who earn their living from writing. Quite often, an editor will want a story by a certain date and the writer may not feel like writing that particular story at all. Sometimes just knowing a story has to be written by lunchtime can make it difficult to even get started. Yet it's no use making excuses, for the writer knows it has to be done.

Readers and advertisers expect the magazine or newspaper to be printed or on line on a specific date.

A writer who told the editor, 'Sorry, I can't write this story you want, I'm not in the mood,' would be looking for another job.

When a writer is having difficulty writing a story, a plan is helpful.

And quite often when writers say they don't write to plans or outlines, what they really mean is they don't work out on paper or one screen what is going to happen in their stories from beginning to end. They certainly KNOW where their first sentence is going to lead and how events will come together. They have a CONCEPT of the whole story. They are so experienced at what they are doing, or writing comes easily for them, so they don't need a formal step-by-step guide.

Plans are a good idea for anyone who has difficulty putting a story together — and perhaps even for those who don't. Once I found myself with a dragon in a three-storey block of flats and no idea what to do with it next. I worked on a whole book that way, never knowing what was going to happen from chapter to chapter. It was the first junior novel I wrote, and I learned that a solution will always suggest itself if you wait long enough. I also learned it is not the best way to write a book, so now I always have a story plan, even if it is mostly in my head.

Of course, if words are chasing each other through your mind at an incredible rate, don't worry about plans. Just write down your story as quickly as you can, then work on it later.

MAKING YOUR STORY PLAN

ONCE YOU HAVE AN idea you want to build into a story, let it brew for a while like tea in a pot.

There probably won't be time to do this in class. But if you allow your ideas to grow at other times, fertilising them with questions until they are big enough to work with, when you do have to write a story you won't have to think about it. If you have been keeping an ideas book or just storing your ideas away in a corner of your mind, you will be able to use one you've already been encouraging to develop.

When you feel you have something to work with, write it down briefly.

At this stage, all you are doing is working out an OUTLINE of your story, so it won't include a lot of detail. That comes later when you start your real writing. All you need to do now is put something down on paper so you can see whether it is going to work as a story.

It may go something like this:

It is just getting dark one night when Hewzie, Jenny, Butch, Keef and Jo are playing cricket in the street. Hewzie slogs their only cricket ball right across the vacant lot into the yard of an old house that is supposed to be haunted. It was old Brubeckermen's place and he was dead three weeks before they found him sitting there with the mouldy crusts of his last meal still on a chipped china plate on his lap. One night when Butch was sneaking to Hewzie's place after bedtime to borrow a homework book he saw a ghostly face staring out of one of the broken windows. The gang will have to get the ball back — but no one will go except Jenny. She seems to be taking a long time. A scream is followed by a crash and when she comes back she says there's a monster under the house. They all decide to go together to fetch the ball, and arm themselves with branches, bricks and broken tiles. When they attack the monster it rushes past them, yowling. 'Cats!' says Hewzie and they all go back home.

Or it could be far simpler:

Jake goes to visit his friend Pete. As he passes the bank, a masked man carrying a bag runs out and takes off along the street. Jakes gives chase, follows the bankrobber into a deadend street, flings his parka over the robber's head and sits on him until the police arrive.

A DIFFERENT STORY

SOMEONE WHO WANTED TO build a bicycle shed in the back yard wouldn't need the same sort of plan as a person who was gong to build a large shopping centre.

There are many different kinds of story and the same kind of storyplan wouldn't work with all of them.

If you are going to write about something that has actually happened, you don't need an outline. You do need a plan of how you are going to present all the facts in an interesting way.

It will be much easier to organise your thoughts if you first divide your story into three separate sections.

An introduction — in which you will let your reader know what your story is about. This can be as short as one simple sentence or as long as several paragraphs. It depends on the final length of your story.

A middle — which will contain most of the information you want to include, the action that takes place and the development of your characters. It will be the biggest part of your story and will be divided into as many smaller sections as you need.

A conclusion — which will tie up any loose ends and finish your story.

Suppose your English grandparents came to stay with your family for five weeks and you wanted to write about it. You had never seen them before and all your other relatives were also overseas.

The first you know about the visit is arriving home from school one afternoon to find your mum waltzing your baby sister around the kitchen table and giggling like a ten-year-old. No milk. No cookies. No `How was school today?'

But there is an airmail letter on the kitchen table where the afternoon tea should be and that explains everything. Nana and Pop are arriving in just three weeks for a five-week visit. Wow!

There is absolute pandemonium in the days that follow. Mum and Dad decide the loose verandah boards and the peeling bedroom ceilings ought to have something done about them. The cupboards get a cleanout and the collection of dead bugs you were keeping on the dressing table is thrown out, along with the wonderful finds of the last ten years you had in the box under your bed.

It's like waiting for Christmas but at last the big day arrives and you wonder whether you'll know yopur grandparents when they get off the plane.

Then there's the visit itself. You have to give up your room and your bed and set up camp in a sleeping bag on the lounge room floor but it's fun. You all go so many places it's like a guided tour of Our Home Town.

At last it's time for them to go home again and everyone's sad. But you've decided it's your turn for a visit next and you're already saving your pocket money. Whew! So much to write down. Where do you start? With a plan — and it would look like this:

Intro: Letter — they are coming.

Middle:
    a. preparation and waiting
    b. the arrival
    c. What we did.
    d. The departure

End: Our turn next. Saving for return visit.

If you really needed to, you could jot down more details to remind yourself what you planned to include in your story. Single words could be enough to jog your memory. eg. *dancing* for the part where your mum was celebrating the good news; *Xmas*, as a reminder of how the waiting seemed.

AN ASSIGNMENT

YOU WOULD PLAN AN assignment in the same way — but with one important difference. Usually you won't know enough about your topic unless you do some research and this will have to be done before you begin the writing. When you do need to research a story, keep these points in mind:

1. Take down only the main points about your topic.

2. Leave out anything that is not important to your story.

If you carefully copy out whole paragraphs from online sites or reference books you will find yourself with so much information you won't know where to start. A list of simple notes written briefly will be much easier to sort into an appropriate order and expressed in your own words.

A NEWS STORY

A NEWS STORY LETS people know what has happened. It must offer the information in a way that will be easily understood by readers from all different backgrounds. The story is told as briefly and simply as possible and nothing unnecessary is included.

Yet whether the writer uses six or thirty sentences to do this, it will be complete in itself. It will have a **beginning** to catch your attention, a **middle** section which contains the information, and a **conclusion** to close it off neatly.

When you come to write your own news stories you can use the three-part story plan we used before. There is also another approach that works well with this type of story. What you do is ask yourself questions about what has happened and then answer them. The key words are *what, when, where, who* and *how?*

It works like this:

What happened?

A BURGLAR WHO TRIED TO STEAL A COLLECTION OF PRICELESS HEIRLOOM JEWELLERY LAST NIGHT WAS FOILED BY A 97-YEAR-OLD GREAT GRANDMOTHER.

When it happened has also been answered in the above sentence.

Who was involved and where did it happen?

MRS MAI BROWNE OF AFGHAN AVENUE, ACACIA VALLEY SURPRISED AN INTRUDER IN HER BEDROOM WHEN SHE RETURNED FROM A BINGO GAME TO CHECK ON A SICK CAT.

How did it happen?

MRS BROWNE, WHO LIVES ALONE WITH HER FIVE BURMESE CATS, SAID SHE WAS A CREATURE OF HABIT.

'USUALLY YOU CAN SET YOUR CLOCK BY ME, BUT I WAS WORRIED ABOUT OTTO,' SHE SAID.

MRS BROWNE ATTACKED THE INTRUDER WITH HER HANDBAG BUT WAS OVERPOWERED AND LEFT LYING ON THE KITCHEN FLOOR WITH HER WRISTS AND ANKLES BOUND.

DETERMINED TO RECOVER THE JEWELLERY WHICH HAD BEEN IN HER FAMILY FOR 500 YEARS, MRS BROWNE WAITED UNTIL THE BURGLAR LEFT THE HOUSE THEN USED HER TOES TO UNTIE HER WRISTS.

SHE DIALLED THE POLICE WHO PICKED UP THE BURGLAR SEVERAL STREETS AWAY AS HE WAS CLIMBING A BRICK WALL.

What **will happen next?**

TOM BAXTER, UNEMPLOYED TRUCK DRIVER OF WEST BANKSIA, HAS BEEN CHARGED AND WILL APPEAR IN COURT THIS MORNING.

How did he find out about the jewellery?

POLICE CONSTABLE JOHN JONES SAID BAXTER READ ABOUT THE JEWELLERY IN THE LOCAL NEWSPAPER.

A conclusion to round off the story:

CONSTABLE JONES SAID MRS BROWNE PLAYED AN AMAZING PART IN CAPTURING THE THIEF.

'NOT AT ALL' SAID MRS BROWNE. 'IN MY YOUNGER DAYS I WAS A CONTORTIONIST WITH LIPMAN'S CIRCUS TROUPE. THEY CALLED ME LADY ELASTIC.'

Notice how some of the questions were asked more than once; and that some sentences could easily be cut if there wasn't enough space to run the full story. This happens a lot when writing for print newspapers.

Accuracy is essential. Double-check all your information. Take nothing for granted, particularly the spelling of names. The great grandmother in our story wouldn't be very happy if you called her Miss May Brown of Arcadia Vale and said she was a former dancer.

Whatever plan you use for your story, you should have a clear idea of how to proceed.

- ☑ Most writers plan their stories, though sometimes this might not be on paper.

- ☑ It helps to have a plan if you want to build a story from an idea. It will be easier to write your story if you know what is going to happen in it.

- ☑ A plan can be brief or detailed.

- ☑ Different kinds of stories require different plans, but every story will have a beginning, a middle and an end.

# TRY THIS...

Write a story plan for one of the following:

A. An assignment.

B. A news story.

C. An account of something that has really happened to you.

D. An imaginary adventure.

When you have written your story plan, READ IT THROUGH CAREFULLY.

Does your plan make sense?

Have you noted all the points you want to include?

You might need to alter the sequence of some of the sections.

Rearrange and adjust your storyplan until you are satisfied you have something to work from.

· 5 ·

WORD PICTURES

IF YOU WERE GOING to work on a picture of your front garden, or a gnarled, crooked tree with naked branches against the background of a wintry sky, first you would sketch in the outlines.

But the world around us is not composed of lines around spaces and you would try to convey that by using colour to fill in the spaces and give them substance.

Writing stories is like making pictures, except we use words instead of paint, crayon or coloured pencil to make them seem real to the reader. An outline is just that and you will need to fill it in, give it shade, tone and depth to imply life.

For the time it takes them to read it, you will want to involve your readers intensely in what you have written. You will want to interest them, entertain them, hold their attention. You will want them to respond in some way: to laugh, to cry, to gnaw their fingernails as the grotesque monster puursues small Paul through the deserted city streets after dark.

Above all, you will want your readers to care about your characters, perhaps even to wonder afterwards whether events really took place, or to feel a sense of loss that the world they have shared temporarily is no more.

That's no easy task. How are you going to go about it?

1. You have to feel something about what you are writing.

You have to be interested, to care about your characters yourself. If you don't, it's highly unlikely your readers will, either, no matter how well you write your story.

2. Choose the words which will best express what you want to say.

There are always many different ways of saying exactly the same thing. You won't be able to try all of them — it would take so long to work out the first sentence there would never be a second or third. It would all be too much like hard work and that is no way to enjoy storywriting.

Here are some points to keep in mind:

A. The simplest way of saying what you want to say is usually the best.

B. Many words don't necessarily make a better story than a few words, just a longer one.

C. The shorter your story, the more important it is to include only what is absolutely necessary.

Writing the best story you can is not something anyone can really teach you. You have to work it out for yourself and that comes from practice, from writing many stories and finding out what sounds right and what does not.

It also helps to read — often. By reading what other people have written you can discover what you enjoy yourself. You can also take note of how they have put their story together and whether it `works'. What sort of words have they used? How long are their sentences? Where does the story begin, and how? How do they move from one incident to another in a way that is interesting and exciting? These are all aspects of a story you will absorb without being aware of it. And, almost automatically, you will begin to use them when you write your own stories.

If you aren't exposed often enough to written language, you won't know how to use it well. It would be like suddenly having to use a computer if you had never seen one being used and didn't know how it worked. If you are going to write stories, then you have to read stories of every possible variety. It's as simple as that.

- ✓ Writing stories is like making pictures. Words are used instead of paint and crayons to fill in story outlines and give them shade, tone and depth.

- ✓ An artist puts in many hours of practice to become skilled at creating pictures. You will need to practise different ways of using words to help your readers 'see' what is happening in your stories.

 **TRY THIS...**

1. 'Paint' a picture of your front garden in words.

2. Describe how it would look at a different time of year.

3. Describe a garden on an imaginary world.

.6.

MAKING WRITING EXCITING

LET'S RETURN TO YOUR story, which has grown from the tiny seed of an idea to a brief outline that you want to build into a complete story Your main character — let's call her Julie — woke up at 9am on Monday, brushed her teeth at 9.30 after having an enormous breakfast of two fried eggs, three grilled sausages, one medium orange juice and two cups of coffee, each with three spoonsful of white sugar. At 9.45 she put on blue jeans, a short-sleeved white T-shirt with Zapped!

written across the front of it, and a pair of brown leather sandals with three straps across the toe and one around the heel. Then at 10am she picked up her brown leather bag and went out of the front door.

Hold it right there! Does your reader really want a minute-by-minute account of Julie's daily life? Or is your reader far more interested in knowing where Julie is going and why, what sort of person she is, and what happened perhaps yesterday that has something to do with what is going to happen today? And what is going to happen now that will set this particular day apart from every other day that has gone before?

As the writer, you have to ask yourself that. And it makes sense to ask yourself those questions before you start writing. We expect something to happen in stories. It would take an exceptional writer to create a gripping story in which little actually happened. Most of us are not that skilful so we have to depend upon action of some kind to arouse our readers' interest. And we have to write about what happens in a way that will sustain that interest throughout our story.

Words are the tools you are going to use to write your story and you will need to really put them to work to make it interesting, exciting, lively and enjoyable.

Words are not merely *said*. They are *murmured, whispered, uttered, screeched, screamed, croaked,* or *whined*. People *holler, yell, shout, giggle, chuckle, shriek, wail, complain, protest*. They *leap, jump, dive, hop, stagger, stumble, creep, tiptoe, hurry, scramble, dawdle, wander* and *hobble*, as well as walk and run.

All you need to do is choose from the vast selection of words at your disposal. Remember, you are using them to colour your picture. You want to make it real. You want to bring it to life. Even if you are writing about something that could never happen you have to write about it in a way that will convince your readers it is actually happening.

The way you describe how a person does something ordinary can make a difference.

If you wanted to tell your readers that Jane made her bed, you could describe how she made it. Meticulously, reluctantly, haphazardly, angrily, thoughtfully? Whichever word you choose to use tells your readers something about Jane and has them wondering why she felt that way. Or instead of using an adverb to describe how she made her bed, you could get creative.

Your readers want to know about the people in your stories. They want to know what they look like, how they think, how they feel. A name is not enough. You are more than your name. You are a unique combination of physical characteristics, attitudes, ideas, thoughts, feelings and responses to situations.

You have a past. Your characters must, too. What has happened to you during all your yesterdays has helped make you who you are today. While you are writing your stories you have to convince your readers your characters also have been influenced in some way by their own yesterdays. You have to make them believe your Jane, whether she is nine or ninety-nine, didn't arrive suddenly from nowhere to take part in some action over a week or a year, only to disappear again just as mysteriously aftrwards.

You have to make Jane live by telling your readers as much as you can about her. But don't spend so long describing Jane and who she is that your reader loses interest in what happens next. You don't have to tell your readers everything. They are quite capable of working out some things for themselves, provided you supply them with information to work from.

1. Build up pictures of your characters through what they have to say and how they say it.

2. Let them reveal things about each other in their conversations.

3. Use actions to provide information. Mention that Jane's hair whipped about in the wind, instead of saying it was long and loose. Have Julie standing on tiptoe to kiss her Mum on the cheek rather than describing her as short.

4. Put yourself right inside your characters. Think and feel for them. They are your puppets. Without you, they can do nothing.

LANGUAGE ALIVE

LANGUAGE IS CONSTANTLY CHANGING. The way we use some words today is different from the way our parents or grandparents would have used them. We rarely notice this change process because we are part of it. But read a book written 500 years ago and you will see that English has changed dramatically over the centuries. Why does it change?

Language is a tool we use to express ourselves to others. Like any other tool, it needs to be updated at times to do a better job. New words are needed to describe inventions and discoveries. We share our lives with others whose languages are different and gradually adapt some of their words for our own use. Long words are conveniently shortened and slang expressions replace everyday words.

No one can ever know a language completely. There will always be a word or phrase that is new to us. We may be able to understand its meaning from the way it is used and from the words which surround it; or we may have to look up its meaning or ask the person who used it. Once exposed to that word, we file it away in our already tremendous mental storehouse of information for future reference.

Every word we add to that storehouse increases our word power.

INCREASING YOUR WORDPOWER

YOU DON'T HAVE TO wait for chance introductions to new words and phrases to build up your wordpower. A person who wants to increase muscle strength can begin a weight training program. You can undertake your own wordpower development program.

1. Learn a new word every day. There are lots of dictionaries online if you don't have one at home.

2. If you come across a word you don't understand, find out its meaning.

3. Have a competition with yourself to see how many words you can come up with in place of *said, walked* and *laughed*.

Set yourself a goal and award yourself a prize, even if it is only a jelly bean you would have eaten anyway, or a TV programme you regularly watch.

4. Observe the world around you and practise describing what you see and hear.

What do clouds look like? How does grass sound when it's walked on after rain? How do trees move in a storm? How would your describe your teacher? Your mum and dad? The old man with the walking stick you saw in the fish and chip shop while you were waiting for your order? You don't have to write anything down. Thinking about it will do.

5. Put your feelings into words, once again not necessarily on paper.

The stronger your wordpower the easier your stories will be to write, and the more interesting they will be to read.

- [x] Language is the writer's tool. Stories are interesting and exciting when it has been used well.

- [x] Language changes all the time. Like any other tool it needs to be updated to do a better job.

- [x] No one ever knows a language completely. We are always learning something new.

- [x] New words and phrases help build stronger wordpower. The stronger your wordpower, the better your stories will be.

 **TRY THIS...**

1. How many different ways can you put this information into words?

Every day on the way to school Meg Lewis passes an old house everyone thinks is empty. One day Meg gets caught in the rain and decides to shelter there. She finds out an old woman who has wandered away from a nursing home is living there. The woman is hungry, confused and afraid. Meg returns her to her family.

2. Make a list of slang words you use every day with your friends. Ask your parents and your grandparents what words they used to say the same thing when they were your age and compare the three lists to see how language has changed.

AN EXTRA ACTIVITY

Start a **wordpower** notebook:

1. Make a note of anything at all that interests you or catches your attention.

It may be the way the sunlight is setting raindrops sparkling on tree leaves after a downpour, or the sound of water going down the plughole. Perhaps on a Sunday drive you passed a crumbling building in a paddock carpeted with green grass, or walked to school on a morning so misty the houses and trees ahead of you were nothing more than an indistinct haze.

2. Try to describe how it looked and how you felt.

You may one day be able to include the information in something you are writing. It helps make stories more believable if you can include details such as how the street looks after rain, or how clothes feel against your skin when you've been drenched in a downpour.

3. Check out the details.

If you're writing about something that happens at eight o'clock one October evening, find out how light it is at that time of night. Are the street lights on? How close would people have to be to recognise each other?

It's no good having Sam or Jodie know from the other side of the street that the person loitering outside Mrs Jackson's deli is the wanted bankrobber Scarface Magee if you've already said there's a power blackout and a thick fog.

Your story doesn't have to have happened but it does have to be realistic enough for your reader to believe it could have.

If you don't remember how it feels to walk on wet grass in bare feet, try it. Then you can write about it. If your story is about

Tansy sitting hiding in a cupboard in an old house while mysterious heavy footsteps are approaching, ask someone to stomp along outside your bedroom door while you sit in the wardrobe to get a sense of how it would be.

Of course you can't try everything that happens in your story to get an accurate sense of how it feels. That's where imagination and wordpower play their part.

· 7 ·

WHAT SORT OF STORY?

AS YOUR IDEA HAS been growing and your storyplan has been taking shape, the type of story will also have suggested itself.

It can be:

>funny or sad
>
>lighthearted or serious
>
>an adventure
>
>a mystery
>
>a chilling spook story

There are as many different kinds of story as there are writers to write them. There are also different styles of writing to suit different stories, just as there are different styles of clothing to suit different occasions.

Some stories are written almost in everyday language as you use it to talk to your family and friends. It's as if the writer has just come around for a chat with you. This book is written in that `conversational style'. It's a style which particularly suits lighthearted or funny stories, magazine articles and books for young people. Because it is similar to our everyday language it's easy to read, easy to write and very much a case of `just talking on paper'.

Other stories are written quite differently and you wouldn't think for a moment that the writer actually speaks that way. We don't normally go into great detail in our conversations, though we might colour an account of an incident with some brief description of characters and place.

For example, I would never say:

Sara shut the door firmly and pushed Ben before her into the cold, driving rain without a backward glance. Trembling raindrops shimmer-tipped the malaleucas. Hibiscus flowers littered the drive like discarded sodden tissues. Sara, head down, did not notice.

Or:

Colin rapped lightly on the window pane to attract the attention of two gaudy twenty eights. They interrupted their possessive stroll along an overhanging wattle tree branch to cock their heads inquisitively for a moment or two. Then they were off in a flash of green brilliance that scattered a shower of bright water gems.

That was what I wrote, but this is probably what I would have said:

Sara pushed Ben out into the pouring rain without looking back.

and

Colin spotted a couple of twenty eights in the wattle tree and tapped on the window. They stopped still for a minute, then they were off.

Listen to the way people tell you about what has happened. Description in everyday speech is not as detailed as that used in stories. Comments made by others are repeated, but they are rarely exact quotes. This is partly because it is impossible to remember precisely everything that has been said, and also because it would take too long. What we tend to do in our conversations is condense and abbreviate comments before we repeat them.

DIRECT AND INDIRECT SPEECH

WHEN WRITERS QUOTE EXACTLY what a character is saying in a story it is called direct speech. This is an example of direct speech:

'I want chips,' said Lindy.

Louisa set her straight. 'The Riviera doesn't have chips on Tuesdays, you dummy, now just hold onto my hand and stop jumping around, you're not Pippi Longstocking.'

'She could have a pie from Charlie the grocer,' Cam suggested.

Mrs Murphy frowned at him and shook her head. 'I think we'll just settle for sandwiches all round, thank you Cam, I don't want everyone going off in all different directions.'

Exactly what each character is saying is included in the story.

This is an example of the same conversation written in indirect speech:

Lindy wanted chips and Louisa had to remind her the Riviera didn't sell chips on Tuesdays. She told Lindy to stop jumping around like Pippi Longstocking. Cam suggested a pie from Charlie the grocer, but Mrs Murphy decided sandwiches all round was the best idea. She didn't want everyone going off in all different directions.

The author reveals what is happening without actually quoting any of the characters.

Points to note:

1. Some stories do not use direct speech and rely entirely on description of events, people and places. Blocks of descriptive writing without direct speech are called narrative.

2. Others tell the whole story with direct speech between the characters.

3. Most are a balance of both narrative and direct speech.

The style in which a story is written is responsible for its mood or atmosphere. Writers select different styles of writing according to what they are working on and the mood they want to create.

The style you choose to use for your stories is up to you.

- ✓ Writers use different styles of writing to suit different stories.

- ✓ Some stories are written almost in everyday language as if the author has called in for a chat.

- ✓ Other stories use language quite differently from the way we use it in everyday speech.

- ✓ When a writer quotes exactly what a character is saying in a story it is called *direct speech*.

- ✓ *Indirect speech* is a way of telling readers what is being said without actually quoting the characters.

- ✓ Descriptive passages without direct speech are called *narrative*.

- ✓ Most stories are a balance of *narrative* and *direct speech*.

TRY THIS...

1. Go to your home bookshelf or the local library and find examples of

   a. A book written in a `conversational' style.

   b. A book written in a very `formal' style.

2. Rewrite the following examples of indirect speech as direct speech.

   a. Jason said he couldn't go to the beach with Jim because his mum wanted him to help clean the yard.

   b. Susie asked if there was any milk in the fridge for her cornflakes.

   c. Tanya said her purse had been taken from her backpack. She wanted to know if anyone had seen the person who stole it.

d. Luke and Ellie thought it would be a lovely day for a picnic. They invited their friends Naomi and Paul to suggest a place to go, but Naomi thought the movies would be a better idea. She said last night's weather update on TV had forecast rain early in the afternoon.

.8.

WHO'S TELLING THE STORY?

EVERY STORY HAS A storyteller aside from the person who wrote it. It can be one of the characters or an unidentified narrator. From this storyteller we learn everything there is to know about our characters and what is happening to them. This is known as the viewpoint.

Two common viewpoints are *first person* and *third person*.

In a story with a first person viewpoint the writer temporarily becomes one of the characters in the story, like an actor taking part in a play.

For example:

If it hadn't been for my mum, the summer before I started high school might have been my best ever. The next summer I would be a teenager. For now I was still just a twelve-year-old.

I saw it as an important milestone, like losing that first wobbly front tooth or needing a bra, though I hadn't actually reached that stage yet.

'You're a late developer, that's all,' Mum reassured me, but I decided I was passing through a transitionary stage nonetheless. I also decided to stop being called Sam and stop chewing my nails.

I was also going to stop being an only child, though that wasn't my decision. In just eight weeks' time, when school started, I would be an older sister.

(From my unpublished manuscript, Wondermother.)

I haven't been twelve years old for longer than I care to remember and my name is Teena, not Samantha. But while I was writing that piece I was Samantha Jones, age 12, commonly known as Sam, who had just had a most unlikely summer holiday. Her mother, eight weeks before presenting Sam with a baby brother, suddenly developed superpowers and complicated everything.

This is the same piece written in the third person:

If it hadn't been for Mrs Jones, the summer before Sam started high school might have been her best ever. The next summer she would be a teenager. For now, she was still just a twelve-year-old.

Sam saw it as an important milestone, like losing the first wobbly front tooth, or needing a bra, though she hadn't actually reached that stage yet.

'You're a late developer, that's all,' Mrs Jones reassured her, but Sam decided she was passing through a transitionary stage between childhood and adolescence nonetheless. She also decided to stop being called Sam, and to stop chewing her nails.

Sam was also going to stop being an only child, though that wasn't her decision.

See the difference?

In the first piece I am Sam, one of the characters in the story. In the second, I am an observer. Both pieces have been written in much the same style but the viewpoint is different. As the writer, I make that decision.

When you write your story, will you be a spectator — or a makebelieve participant?

PUTTING YOU IN YOUR STORY

If you put yourself into your story you don't have to be yourself as you are now. Cast yourself in any role that appeals to you.

Be a crippled crooked old crone with a face like crumpled paper and legs like twisted matchsticks.

Be a completely unbalanced old man with the crazy idea that burning all the money in the world on a huge bonfire would solve all our problems.

Be a tiny girl...a hassled mum...an impatient dad.

Don't forget, you don't have to be human. You can choose to be an animal or even an alien.

Becoming temporarily what you are not allows you to give your stories a completely different angle. It provides greater scope for your ideas — a wider canvas on which to paint your picture.

If you are in your story, in whatever shape or form, then you have to BE there in every sense of the word.

If you are the crippled old crone you can't say *I ran at top speed to catch the bus before it pulled out.* If you are old and crippled you never run at top speed. You have to hobble, to make your way with great difficulty — and frustration, too, that your body can no longer do what you want.

The tiny girl, the hassled mum and the impatient dad will each have a different view of the same situation.

For the time it takes you to write your story, you have to see what is happening from the viewpoint of the person you have chosen to be. It is like acting in a play, only you have to write your own lines. What would you say if you were that person?

What would you do? How would you think and feel?

No one is watching you perform but how convincing a part you play in your story will determine whether it is believable.

- [x] Every story has a storyteller aside from the writer.
- [x] The reader learns what is happening from this imaginary person's viewpoint.
- [x] The writer pretends to be one of the characters in a story with a first person viewpoint.
- [x] The writer takes the role of an observer in a story with a third person viewpoint.
- [x] Writers can take on any role in a story and write it from that character's viewpoint.

# TRY THIS...

1. Select a book from the library and read the first chapter. What viewpoint has the writer chosen to use? Is it immediately obvious or do you have to think about it? If the author has chosen to use the first person, is the character believable?

2. Rewrite the first page of the book you've selected using a different viewpoint.

3. Two school friends discover a briefcase full of money in a laneway and take it to the police after first arguing about what to do with it. Write a story casting yourself as

    a. The person who lost the briefcase.

    b. One of the two friends.

    c. The duty police officer at the station.

· 9 ·

LET'S BEGIN...

PLUNGE YOUR READER RIGHT into your story — and not necessarily at the logical beginning. Start right in the middle of the action, if you like. Let your main character be hot on the heels of a masked bank robber right in the first sentence. That way you will 'hook' your readers' attention so they want to find out what happens next.

If you begin like this it won't be very interesting:

Jake woke up in the morning and asked his mum if it was okay if he went out for a walk and called in to see Pete. His mum said it was all right but he had to wear his coat because it was raining. He put on his coat, opened the door and went out.

You can leave it right till the end of the story to tell your reader Jake was going to see Pete:

Inspector Evans clapped Jake on the back in congratulation.

'You've nabbed yourself a bank robber, my boy. Top notch!'

Jake grinned. 'And all I set out to do was visit my best friend, Pete!'

You don't need to say that Jake woke up in the morning. Of course he did or he wouldn't be out there on the street. If Jake couldn't wake up in the usual way one morning, that would be something out of the ordinary and the beginning of an interesting story. Your reader would want to know why. To find out, they would have to read on.

Story beginnings must grab your readers' interest and hold it. You don't want them to wonder whether to go roller skating or bike riding after school in between reading the first and second sentence. You want them to read your story right through from start to finish.

Beginnings that plunge readers right into the action, raise questions, or suggest that something is going to happen encourage them to do this.

For example:

Zoe froze. Someone was coming. She shouldn't be here.

This dives right into the action as well as raising questions. Who is coming? Where is Zoe? What is she doing there? What is going to happen now?

An opening sentence like *Paul had already decided not to like the house on the corner* will have your readers wondering why and arouse their curiosity about the connection between Paul and the house.

If Lori had gone straight home from school the way she was supposed to, things would have been different lets them know immediately that something changed because she didn't go straight home from school.

By beginning with, *As soon as Pete reached the front gate he knew something was wrong,* your readers will have to read on if they want to find out what it was and why Pete was alerted to it at the front gate.

Direct speech can also be used for beginnings that draw readers right into the action. Here are two examples that raise questions and suggest something is going to happen:

1. 'Come on,' urged John, plunging through the undergrowth. 'They'll be after us.'

Susie lurched to a halt and sagged against a burnt tree trunk, struggling for breath before gasping, 'It's no use, I can't.'

We want to know who is chasing them, why they are being chased and if they will manage to escape.

2. *'My dad will have to go,' Luke McAlister told his best friend Alex Jackson on the way home from school the Thursday before the summer holidays started. Shoulders hunched, hands dug deep into the pockets of his shorts, he kicked a rock. 'I've had enough of him. He's the meanest, crankiest dad any kid could have.'*

This was the way I started *Mad Dad For Sale*, and it instantly tells the reader that Luke has a problem with a cranky dad. How will he solve it?

.10.

CARRY ON...

WHAT COMES NEXT? IF you've thought out your story carefully and are working from a plan you will know what you want to say. You've jumped the first hurdle and made a start. Even the longest journey begins with the first step and you are on your way. All you have to do is continue. This is where your wordpower will be operating at maximum strength.

You need to show your readers what you have created in your mind. To make your mental images become mind pictures for others you will be using words to colour your stories. Some colours are brighter and stronger than others. So are some words.

You can use *thrust* instead of *put*, *hurled* instead of *threw*, *toppled* instead of *fell*.

Some words suggest the sounds they are describing: *sighing, wailing, moaning, groaning. Spluttered, chattered, splashed* and *hissed*. These are the sorts of words that can bring your stories to life.

Sentence length also creates different moods. Very short, simple sentences move stories along at top speed. They are ideal for chases, action and danger.

Check this out:

But they had to move on. And now. Already agitated barking was shattering the stillness. Harsh shouts punctuated the birdcalls. Their escape had been discovered. Reaching the town by nightfall was their only hope.

Susie folded to her knees. 'Leave me.'

John hesitated. She was a liability. Alone, he could make it, bring help, rescue the others. But leave her here? Abandon her to their mercy? No!

He hauled her roughly to her feet. 'Move!'

'I can't!' The wail of protest was ignored.

He plunged forwards, dragging her with him. Branches scratched their faces, tugged at their clothing. Tree roots tripped them. They stumbled, staggered onwards. With a strength born of desperation they forced their way through the reluctant forest.

This continues the story begun in the last section. Words are kept to an absolute minimum. Does it work? You decide.

Longer sentences don't necessarily slow down the action of a story.

Joshua gave the loudest groan he possibly could, did a triple somersault over the back of the sofa, tunnelled under the table right through his gran's legs, dived out of the front door and slid down three bannisters one after the other until he reached the footpath outside.

This could be divided into several shorter sentences, but I wanted to give an impression of boundless energy that left a feeling of breathlessness.

Use colourful words and appropriate sentence lengths to create mood and atmosphere.

IN ADDITION

AVOID WRITING STORIES THAT sound like a list of events.

This is boring:

He walked into the room. He looked into the corner. He saw a chair. He went over and sat down. He felt tired. He closed his eyes.

The reader will probably feel like taking a doze if the story continues at this pace. It isn't moving along in an interesting way and every sentence begins with the same word.

This sounds better:

Immediately Sam walked into the room the chair in the corner attracted his attention. It looked comfortable and inviting. Zoe was right, he suddenly realised. He was tired. The last few hours had taken their toll. Surely it wouldn't hurt to take a short nap.

The same thing is happening in both paragraphs, but in the second version the picture is clearer. The reader has to work out a few things, but that's a good way of holding attention.

LINKS IN A CHAIN

STORIES HAVE TO FLOW. Events must move easily and effortlessly one into another. Our own lives seem to progress in a steady step-by-step sequence, from minute to minute and action to action. Stories are more interesting if we increase the pace, leap from place to place, skip from time to time. This is done with link words and sentences and by including only what is necessary.

Using the time to move stories along results in the list effect mentioned earlier.

Your main character wakes up at 7am, has breakfast at 7:30, is dressed by 8 and leaves for school at 8:15. He meets his friend at 8:45, eats lunch at 12, arrives home at 3:45 and goes to bed at 9pm.

No one will want to read it if you write it all down.

Only mention the time if it is important to the story.

If a kidnapper leaves a note for Mr and Mrs Rich telling them it's goodbye little Tommy unless they leave two million dollars in a paper bag in a rubbish bin at the corner of Lupin and Banksia Streets at midnight on Friday, it's a race with the clock. The time will need to be mentioned throughout the story so the reader knows whether the Riches will save their son.

In stories where the precise time of an event is unimportant, use other ways to indicate that time has passed.

Here are some examples:

It was nearly dawn before Jed finally slept.

That evening I prepared myself for the journey ahead.

After a restless night, Tony crawled listlessly out of bed to face another day that promised to be no better than the last.

During the afternoon, Lisa wrestled anxiously with the problem. She could not concentrate on maths or social studies. She fumbled her way through the crucial match between James High and Larkwood.

By morning, Jodie had made her decision. She would go with Mrs Luke to Darwin. Without pausing to change into her day clothes, she hurried to tell her so.

You don't have to be direct. You can drop hints.

The sun was high overhead when Tania left the homestead for the corral.

This tells your reader it is around midday without your having to say 12pm.

The events in your stories will seem to flow smoothly into one another if you link them with sentence beginnings like this:

Eventually....At long last...Finally....After a while...When...No sooner than...Immediately...At the same time...As...While...By midnight...Meanwhile...

There are many, many more. How many can you think of? All it takes is practice.

.11.

...THE END

A STORY HAS REACHED its end when there is no need to say any more. The more you write and read, the better will be your sense of when and how a story should end.

Here are some pointers:

1. It is a good idea to know how your story will end before you begin it.

You might even want to write your conclusion before your introduction, as I sometimes do.

Don't be afraid to change your ending if you come up with a better one while you are writing.

2. Stories need to draw to a satisfactory close, not jolt to a sudden unexpected halt like a car running out of petrol.

Don't leave your readers feeling as if they've been taken out for a drive and left rudely at the roadside with no hope of reaching their destination. They want to be taken all the way there.

Make it a round trip, if you like and leave your story in almost the same place it began.

It's all right to leave your readers wondering — was there a dragon or wasn't there? Had the Finch family seen the last of the wailing woman who haunted the dining room? Was Julie-ann telling the truth about the gold locket she said she found under the floorboards of Treleaven Manor?

Just make sure your readers aren't left with the feeling, Is that it? How would you feel if you went the movies, watched the commercial and the start of the main feature and were then left watching a blank screen?

3. Answer any questions raised in your story, particularly if it is a mystery or an adventure. Tie up all the loose ends and finish them off neatly as you would on a piece of embroidery, or slot in the final piece of the puzzle to complete the whole picture.

4. You might already have an idea for a new story about the same characters. Use your ending to lay the groundwork and leave your options open for another exciting chapter in their lives.

For example:

I felt a bit sad now it was all over. No more investigation. No more book. Everything finished. But then, maybe not. As Jen said cheerfully when she watched me write INVESTIGATION CLOSED on the 84 May

Street file: 'That's that mystery solved, then. Wonder what our next assignment will be?'

5. Real life is not like fantasy. There are no neat and tidy endings and situations aren't always satisfactorily resolved.

In some stories, the characters don't overcome every obstacle and find final solutions to their problems. There are no villains and heroes, just ordinary people capable of both good and bad behaviour. These stories show that change is a gradual process, always difficult, often painful and growth as a person comes slowly.

- ☑ Story beginnings must 'hook' your readers' attention and hold it.

- ☑ Plunging right into the action, raising questions in the first sentence and suggesting that something exciting is going to happen will do this.

- ☑ Wordpower has to operate at full strength to bring stories to life for your readers.

- ☑ Colourful words and appropriate sentence lengths create mood and atmosphere.

- ☑ Stories are boring if they read like a list of events. Increase the pace, leap from place to place and skip from time to time to make them more interesting.

- ☑ Link words and sentences help stories to flow effortlessly from one event to another.

- ☑ Only include essential information in your stories. If you put in enough clues, your readers will work out the rest for themselves.

- ☑ A story is finished when there is no need to say any more.

TRY THIS...

1. Write three different beginnings for the following story:

Melissa's dad has just got a job in another state and the family will have to move. Melissa doesn't want to go so decides to leave home. Using the babysitting money she has been saving for a new phone, she catches the bus to her grandfather's farm in the country. He talks her into going back home and convinces her the move can be a great adventure.

2. Choose one of your three beginnings to start your story. Continue it, using your strongest wordpower to create an exciting story. Don't forget link words and phrases to step up the pace.

3. Write three different conclusions. Select the one you think best rounds off your story.

. 12 .

HELP WANTED!

WHAT IF YOU CAN'T even start your story, never mind finish it?

A blank sheet of paper is staring you in the face. Time is ticking by. Perhaps you know what you want to write, but nothing you can think of to put down on paper sounds quite the way you want it to.

DON'T WORRY.

Forget that troublesome first sentence. Start on the second, third, fourth, or even the last.

Start wherever you can. It doesn't matter, as long as you put down one sentence that will lead you on to others. You can always come back later and write a beginning.

I write many of my stories from the end or the middle. I write down whatever is clear in my mind: several lines of verse, a few sentences, a paragraph, several pages. Where I start writing it is not important because I know how my story is going to work out. What is important is putting down my ideas while they are fresh in my mind.

When I have a collection of verses, paragraphs or pages, I sort them into their correct sequence, then fill in the gaps to complete my story. It works for me. It could work for you. You need to work in whatever way you feel comfortable.

Perhaps it isn't the beginning that has you stumped. Maybe you are halfway through your story. You really like what you've written so far, but suddenly you've come to a standstill. It's as if someone just turned off your tap of creativity and you can't turn it on again no matter how you try. What do you do?

NOTHING.

Leave your story right there if you can. Put it away. Start another one, take a walk, do something completely different.

Later, when you aren't even thinking about writing, that next sentence will arrive unexpectedly and you will be on your way again.

In class you won't be able to do this and here is where your plan will prove its worth. You've already worked out what is going to happen in your story, so even if you run out of enthusiasm you will still be able to complete it. You might not be 100 per cent happy with what you write, but at least it will be finished. Later, you can rewrite it.

Try talking to a friend about your story. Sometimes this will trigger the flow of ideas far better than sitting staring at a piece of paper.

One writer had the right idea and put this sign above her desk:

- [✓] When you are having problems writing your story, start anywhere you can. Just put something down on paper.
- [✓] Take a break and do something completely different for a while.
- [✓] Talk to a friend about your story.
- [✓] **DON'T WORRY.**

· 13 ·

PRUNING AND SHAPING

A KEEN GARDENER WILL prune and shape a plant that has grown straggly or untidy. Writers do the same thing with their stories.

We are never completely happy with every story we produce and usually consider the first effort a rough draft to be carefully crafted into its final form. We do this by cutting out words or phrases, substituting one word for another, rearranging, changing and rewriting where necessary. This is called EDITING.

First steps:

1. Carefully read through your story. Make sure you read what you have actually written and not what you intended to write.

2. Read your story aloud to find out whether the sentences sound awkward.

3. Insert any punctuation you have missed in your haste to put down your ideas.

4. Check any spellings you're not sure are correct.

You may think these points are unimportant, but the rules of written language do serve a purpose. They are not to make your life difficult but to enable you to express yourself on paper in a way that will be readily understood by others.

What would be the point of someone giving you a story written in heiroglyphics unless you were an ancient Egyptian? When you write a story, you are trying to communicate your ideas to others. There's no point you being the only person who can make sense of it.

The rules of written expression are not rigid. They are a basis for you to work from and there is still plenty of scope for you to say what you want to say in your own special way.

When you have done all you can to make your story understandable, ask yourself what you can do to improve it.

1. Rearrange words, sentences and paragraphs where necessary.

2. Substitute stronger words or more colourful expressions for those you have used.

3. Rewrite the sections you aren't happy with.

4. Where you haven't made yourself quite clear, provide more explanation of the situation. Describe events in greater detail. You know what you had in mind when you wrote your story, but your readers won't if you don't give them enough information to work with.

5. Is every word you have used absolutely necessary — or have you said more than enough? Cross out anything you now consider unnecessary to your story.

6. Make sure you have used the same VIEWPOINT and TENSE throughout your story. Shifting haphazardly between first and third person viewpoint will confuse your readers. If you cast yourself at the beginning as a spectator relating events you can't suddenly take on the role of one of the characters and start writing as though you are actively taking part in everything that is happening.

Experienced writers will often use different viewpoints in long works such as novels, but they do this intentionally to make their story stronger. To do this successfully, you really have to know what you are doing.

Decide before you begin writing your story whether it will be told in the PAST TENSE as something that has already happened, or in the PRESENT TENSE, as a sequence of events that is currently evolving as you write. Then stick to your decision. You will confuse your reader if you keep changing tense.

7. Pay attention to details. If your main character has red hair and freckles on page one, she can't have brown hair and a clear complexion on page three unless she's dyed her hair and discovered a miracle freckle fader. The police constable you introduce in the first paragraph at the scene of the crime can't be a chief superindent by the time he reaches the station in paragraph 10 unless you can offer a good explanation for his lightning promotion.

Here is an example of one section of this book to show you the changes I made to the original draft:

If you ~~wanted to eat peas and had~~ decided to grow ~~some~~ *peas* in your back garden, you wouldn't ~~you'd hardly expect to neglect them completely after sowing your~~ *sow the* seeds *then neglect them* until you felt hungry. ~~Because you know that~~ Seeds only bear fruit given time and the right ~~kind of~~ conditions so you'd do your ~~utmost~~ best to provide these.

Encouraging your story ideas to grow is a little like gardening. Quite often, ideas are ~~only very,~~ very vague to begin with. Many are little more than fleeting ~~fleeting impressions~~ *thoughts*. They are there and they have possibilities, but ~~if~~ they ~~are going to develop into stories we have to provide~~ need the right kind of conditions to develop into stories. Sometimes, if ~~our~~ the idea~~s are~~ is very hardy, all ~~they~~ it need~~s~~ is time. Often, however, time only allows them to wither and die. ~~We~~

~~don't want that to happen, so we~~ *To prevent that happening,* you can fertilise them with questions.

The amount of reworking you do on your own story before you are satisfied will depend on you.

☑ Writers are rarely satisfied with their first attempt at a story.

☑ They prune and shape their stories just as gardeners prune and shape plants to improve their appearance.

☑ Crafting a first draft into its final form is called EDITING.

☑ The aim of a writer is to communicate clearly with the reader, so the first step in editing is to check spelling, punctuation and sentence structure.

☑ When a story is understandable it can then be improved by rearranging or substituting words and sentences and rewriting some sections.

☑ Details such as names and descriptions must also be checked to make sure they are consistent.

TRY THIS...

Edit the following:

A really really quiet street Oleander drive was maybe the quietest in the whole town until Mrs maloney she lived at No 54 in Oleander Drive won the Lotto and the cat burgulars decided to take Oscar and hold him to ransum although her favourite pet had his own ideas about that. elliott and Cassandra don't had any clues about becomming catnappers until they read about Mrs Maloney and Oscar in the Western Crhronicle. Cassandra was looking for an ordinary job elliott is looking for a new car They in the shopping centre carpark when they read the story in the newspapper that told all about Mrs Maloney and Oscar

Mistakes to look for:
- Five spelling mistakes
- A missing word
- Repeated details
- Missing capital letters
- Missing punctuation
- A sentence that is too long and badly constructed
- Changes between past/present tense

(Suggested final edit: Oleander Drive was a very quiet street until Mrs Maloney at Number 54 won Lotto and the cat burglars decided to take Oscar and hold him to ransom. Elliott and Cassandra didn't think of becoming catnappers until they read about Mrs Maloney and her favourite pet in the Western Chronicle. They were in the shopping centre carpark at the time. Cassandra was looking for an ordinary job. Elliott was looking for a new car.

. 14 .

IMAGINATION UNLIMITED

IT'S TRUE YOU CAN'T judge a book by its cover but sometimes presentation will decide whether your story is read. An interesting title and skilful writing won't guarantee this. Your story has to look good too if you want to attract readers.

Tatty pages covered with scrawled handwriting, scratchings out and some of last night's pea soup dinner won't do that. Your rough copy can be in any state as long as you can understand it. But before you offer your story to others, pay some attention to its appearance. After all, it's a reflection of you and you want to make a good impression.

Once you are happy with the final edit of your story you can take the simple approach and rewrite it in your neatest writing on crisp, clean paper or print it out on the computer.

You might like to use your artistic skills, imaginative ideas and whatever materials you have at hand to create something a little out of the ordinary.

Here are a few simple ideas to get you started:

1. Make your own book. Publishing your own work can be fun and your book can be as unusual as you care to make it. Experiment with colour, shape, size and texture. Select from decorative lettering, neat handwriting, typewritten text (words) and computer printout. Paper comes in a rainbow of colours and a variety of weights and textures.

Art supply stores will offer the most exciting range to choose from and it can be fun to browse the shelves or check out what's available online.

You do not have to stick with pen and paper. Why not use some of the specially formulated fabric paints and create a cloth book on silk or linen?

Your illustrations are limited only by your imagination and your artistic ability. Pencil or ink drawings, water colours, poster paints, photographs, collage — the choice is yours. If you consider yourself more of a writer than an artist why not collaborate with a more artistic friend? Many picture books are written by one person and illustrated by another.

2. Make a scroll. This can be an impressive presentation for a poem or short story. Select an interesting sheet of paper, and use fancy lettering. Lettering charts are available from newsagencies and art supply stores, or you could seek out a book on calligraphy and develop your own penmanship skills. Many computer programs offer a range of interesting `fonts' or type styles to choose from, plus some creative borders, and it can be great fun designing your page.

Once you have your story or poem on paper, simply roll it into a tube and tie it with string, yarn or ribbon. If you want to use your scroll as a wall hanging, attach a length of light wood or plastic stripping at each end.

3. Make your sheet of paper into a concertina, so that your story really does unfold. This can be as small as a 5cm square when folded, or as large as you like.

4. Cut your page or pages to a shape related to your story. If your poem is about flowers, cut out the shape of a flower in coloured paper and write the verses on individual petals. If your subject was sausages, cut your paper into sausage shapes, write on them, then string them together in the right sequence and hang them from a `butcher's hook'.

5. `Hex' your story — make a three dimensional hexagon (or cube or pyramid) from board or stiff paper and use the sides as your pages.

. 15 .

STORIES ARE FOR SHARING

FOR AS LONG AS there have been people living together, there has been storytelling in one form or another. Myths, legends, and tales of heroic deeds which were born of an evening by a glowing fire or in a crowded, dusty market place have been passed from person to person throughout the centuries.

They spread by word of mouth to begin with and then, when people began to rely more on writing to communicate, they were written down, so that today we can read them.

People were prepared to share what they had written, so now we can know something of lives and times that are long gone. They gave us this. By allowing your friends to read what you have written, you are giving them something of yourself.

SHOULD YOU SHARE ALL YOUR STORIES?

SOMETIMES OUR WRITING IS unsuitable for sharing, particularly if we've expressed all our hurt, anger and frustration on paper instead of in person. Doing this makes us feel better but this sort of writing is usually personal. It could cause problems if anyone read it. Would you really feel good if your mum and dad knew what you wanted to do to them the week you were grounded for giving your little brother a black eye? Besides, moods pass. The way we feel one day is rarely the way we feel the next.

SHARING CAN BE SCARY

READING YOUR STORY ALOUD to a group can be a real problem if you don't like being the centre of attention, even if the audience is made up of friends. You're not sure how it will be received, and because writing seems such a part of yourself, that matters. You want to be liked, and you want what you have done to be well received.

Even writers who have no problem selling their stories to a magazine or newspaper so that 30,000 strangers can read them can be reluctant to share their work with friends.

COPING WITH CRITICISM

A DIRECT RESULT OF sharing is criticism and that's not easy to accept. It doesn't make any difference whether it's our hair, the way we walk, how we behave or our story that's being criticised. We feel hurt.

If you can listen to what is being said about your story without taking it personally, you can use it to improve your work.

Others will often notice things about your writing you would never have noticed yourself. You may have gone to great lengths to say something that could have been said far more simply. Or you may not have said enough, giving the reader too little to work with. Comments like these can be kept in mind the next time you begin work on a story.

Sharing your stories will let you know also whether your story is having the intended effect. Perhaps your serious story has your audience shrieking with laughter, or your funny story doesn't even raise a smile. If you didn't share your stories, you would never know.

The main thing to keep in mind with criticism is that it is your story being criticised, not you.

Don't forget, also, that opinions will vary. The story one person considers quite brilliant will be found boring by someone else.

Sharing will often attact suggestions. Perhaps the story could have moved in another direction, or the ending could have been different. You might welcome some suggestions and decide to follow through on them. Remember, it is your story. You will want to make it the best story you can but that doesn't mean it needs to be completely changed to suit others' ideas. Everyone will not like what you have written. Some will — and if you do, and feel good about it, that's all that matters.

FINALLY

WE ALL HAVE DIFFERENT skills and abilities and what one person finds easy, another will not. Some of you may still find it much harder to write a story than solve a maths problem or shoot a winning goal. Anyone can try to tell you how to write. No one can do it for you. Only you can do that. Happy writing!

ABOUT THE AUTHOR

Teena Raffa-Mulligan has been having fun with words for as long as she can remember. Her many publications for children include poems, short stories, picture books, junior fiction and middle grade novels. Teena enjoys sharing her love of story telling with people of all ages and encouraging them to write their own stories. She is always happy to hear from young readers and answer their questions about writing.
Email teenawriter@gmail.com

To find out about Teena's books and author visits go to www.teenaraffamulligan.com

www.ingramcontent.com/pod-product-compliance
Lightning Source LLC
Chambersburg PA
CBHW050317010526
44107CB00055B/2274